# Energy for Life

# Energy for Life

### Reflections on a Theme

*"Come, Holy Spirit—*
*Renew the Whole Creation"*

## Krister Stendahl

PARACLETE PRESS
Brewster, Massachusetts

Library of Congress Cataloging-in-Publication Data

Stendahl, Krister.
    Energy for life : reflections on a theme : "Come Holy Spirit, renew the whole creation" / Krister Stendahl. — 2nd ed.
      p.  cm.
    Includes bibliographical references.
    ISBN 1-55725-233-5 (pbk.)
    1. Holy Spirit—Biblical teaching. 2. Holy Spirit Meditations. I. Title.
    BS680.H56 S74 1999
    231'.3—dc21                                          99-34075
                                                              CIP

10  9 8 7 6 5 4 3 2 1

© 1999 by Krister Stendahl
All rights reserved. First edition 1990
Second edition 1999

ISBN 1-55725-233-5

Published by Paraclete Press
Brewster, Massachusetts
www.paraclete-press.com

Printed in the United States of America.

# Table of Contents

v

# Preface

All books have their history, even small ones like this one. The Latin saying *habent sua fata libelli* became proverbial. During a meeting at the World Council of Churches I happened to express enthusiasm over the theme that had been chosen for its Seventh General Assembly, which was to be held in Canberra, Australia, in the winter/summer of 1991. That led to my being asked to write a short book to be read in the churches and by the delegates in preparation for that Assembly. The theme was this: Come Holy Spirit—Renew the Whole Creation.

Those months of meditating, thinking, and finally writing about that theme refreshed my soul and sustained my enthusiasm. Out of it I wrote, and I feared that my readers would find some things strange, some points even wrong, and much of it one-sided. It seems, however, that many found the book helpful. Thus I am deeply grateful when Paraclete press rescues my writing from remaining a now obsolete publication for an Assembly soon ten years back. And it feels as if my little book has come home, for where else would a book on the Holy Spirit belong but with a Press that has chosen its focus and purpose in the word "Paraclete" and that for which it stands. It is John the evangelist who gives the name *parakletos* to the Holy Spirit, and, as so often happens with the Johannine language, words bristle with meanings, all meaningful. That is certainly true in this case: Advocate—Counselor—Helper—Comforter—Intercessor. . . .

In my enthusiasm over the Theme, I wanted to experiment with thinking and writing in "Spirit language," not "Christ language." I did so in the firm conviction that my faith needed to be renewed by the mystery of the Trinity. When we say Holy

Spirit we say God. It is important to put the comma in the right place. God, comma, the Father and the Son and the Holy Spirit. It is not God the Father plus the Son plus the Spirit. It is God the Father, God the Son, God the Holy Spirit in glorious and organic unity.

The Theme opens up the opportunity to exercise and renew our faith by thinking and speaking Spirit language. This I tried. It is just an attempt, with all the flaws of a trial effort. For my own tradition has not been used to such language. I was given to believe that the Holy Spirit was "only" the conveyor and communicator of the gospel and its blessings. It took some time before the words from the Nicene Creed sank in: "I believe in the Holy Spirit, the Lord and Giver of Life. . . ." I was further stimulated when I learned that the Eastern churches did not feel it wise or necessary to have the Spirit defined as proceeding not only from the Father but also "from the Son."

I refer to the so-called *filioque,* added to the creed in the West in the Middle Ages.

That *filioque,* far from being a case of theological hair-splitting, became for me a reminder of how the church at times tends to be over-anxious not to allow the Spirit its free range.

I called the book *Energy for Life.* As I wrote, the word "energy" suggested itself often and naturally.

When I tried to answer the question how I personally experience the Holy Spirit, then the first and clearest answer had to be: as energy. I think it is a good word. I think it is a better word than "power." Power is for ruling. Energy is for living.

*In Holy Week, 1999*
*Krister Stendahl*

# ONE

# The Theme is a Prayer

*Come Holy Spirit—Renew the whole creation* is the Theme for these reflections. The first thing to note is that it is a prayer. The language of prayer is the mother-tongue of faith, and prayer is the heartbeat of religion. Prayer is indeed the language most authentic to the church. Proclamations and declamations, pronouncements and statements abound in this world—political and theological, religious and secular.

But to be given words of prayer, that is to be invited to taste the gift of faith in one's own mouth.

I know a priest in a big city who likes to say, when asked what he would do if he were given a million: "I would buy up advertisement space in the subway stations and there I would put up short, one-line words of prayer." Perhaps like "Come, Holy Spirit—

Renew the Whole Creation." I think he knew how healing it is when the church gives of its most authentic gifts, its language of prayer.

I guess there was a time—before radio and television—when people both in towns and villages were seldom addressed by any other public pronouncements than the mighty sermons in church. But now we all are bombarded by messages through the media. They have even learned to make those messages "subliminal," manipulating us without our knowing, so that we cannot defend ourselves.

In such a situation, the language of prayer comes to us with healing.

That is so because messages—even the good ones—tend to treat us as an audience, or even as consumers. But when given a word of prayer we are invited to practice the most holy art of creativity, to be co-creators with God in Christ. And if I read the Gospels right, Jesus seems to have known better than most how to elicit and awaken faith and action in people rather than making them the passive targets for messages—or even for the Message.

Actually, when we recite our Creeds, we are on the borderline of prayer. I remember well when the Greek Orthodox biblical scholar Father Theodore Stylianopoulos gave the opening address at the Sixth General Assembly of WCC in Vancouver, 1983. The theme that time was the proud proclamation *Jesus Christ—the Life of the World,* but as Father Ted spoke out of his tradition, showing how creeds are "doxological," that is, expressions of praise in gratitude to God, that proclamation took on on a new and different tone. Now we stood before God in awe and worship, with angels and archangels and all the company of heaven, gathering up the hopes of the world in him who is the Logos.

To speak about prayer in this manner may strike some as very pious, but the strange thing is that common folk often understand this matter better than preachers and theologians.

In that homeland of mine, Sweden, people are incredibly shy about their faith. Thus the opinion polls show time and again that considerably larger numbers admit to their praying to God than to their believing in the existence of God. I do not like to condone such shyness but I would rather have it that way than the other way round.

The act of prayer is an act of faith, and it is out of prayer that authentic theology and confession can become articulate, moving dynamically from prayer via doxology towards creeds and theologies. Creeds and theologies do help us to become articulate. They raise our consciousness. They can sharpen our vision for the consequences and possibilities of our faith. They can enliven and give profile to the life of prayer by making us more and more aware of God's possibilities in which justice and grace, law and compassion, creativity and trust all come together in the mystery of the Holy Trinity.

**Come, Holy Spirit . . .**

The Theme is a prayer out of our need. It is an intensified *Kyrie eleison, Christe eleison.* It is a cry out of our helplessness, faithlessness, powerlessness. When everything seems meaningless, when the world hungers for justice and peace, when all the solutions we can think of seem to have their undesirable side-effects for people and for nature, when our imagination runs dry, when our will loses its energy, then we cry: Come, Holy Spirit . . . come and rescue us from the coolness of cynicism and selfishness. For we understand what Jesus meant with his observation that when problems become overwhelming, then most people's love will grow cold (Matt. 24:12), human solidarity will collapse, and people will look after only their own interests. And we cry that the Spirit may deliver us from that desperation that seeks release in fanaticism—not least the religious kind.

*Come,* Holy Spirit. . . . When we think about it, there is something odd about ask-

5

ing the Spirit to *come*. As if the Spirit were not all the time present, ever pervasive, ever penetrating. Perhaps it is rather we who should come, open up to, become aware of the power of the Spirit.

Yet it is one of the gracious signs of God's acceptance of our limitations as creatures that we are allowed, even encouraged, to pray out of our needs and our perceptions without first having to make sure that our language is perfect, or commensurate with the inscrutable mysteries of the divine: "In everything let your requests be made known to God" (Phil. 4:6).

It is good to remember that the apostle Paul also knew how we can become so discouraged that we cannot find words for prayer. Then "the Spirit comes to our help in our weakness; for we do not know how to pray as we ought, but the Spirit itself intercedes for us in sighs without words" (Rom. 8:26).

When we now make bold to pray *Come, Holy Spirit—Renew the Whole Creation,* it

is as if we spoke what is called an *epiklesis,*
i.e., that most holy prayer of sanctification
and even transformation, spoken over earthly
things. And we are called back to our sacred
duty of interceding for the world as the
Spirit intercedes for us according to the will
of God (Rom. 8:27) and witnesses with our
spirit that we are God's children (Rom.
8:16). And Christ in his glory is our intercessor (Rom. 8:34) as we draw near to God
through the one who is our High Priest since
he "always lives to make intercession for
us" (Heb. 7:25).

### The Spirit and the Trinity

Who is a Christian? To me and to many
the obvious answer is: one who believes in
Jesus Christ. That belief can then be defined,
described, and elaborated in all those ways
that make up the spectrum of Christian theology. It seemed so obvious to me. You
could even hear it in the name: Christ—
Christians. Of course I knew from the Acts
of the Apostles (11:26) that presumably it

was the outsiders who came up with the name, and that it was not really the church's chosen self-designation—a little like the name "Quakers" for the Society of Friends. But that made no difference. A Christian, for me, was one who believed in Jesus Christ.

Undoubtedly our identity as Christians rests in Christ. But when I met other Christians, and especially those shaped by Eastern Orthodox traditions, I learned that there was a better and fuller way of answering the question: Who is a Christian? That answer is: A Christian is one who believes and worships the Triune God. Let me quote the beginning of a classical collect for the Sunday of the Holy Trinity:

> Almighty and ever-living God, you have given us grace, by the confession of true faith to acknowledge the glory of the eternal Trinity, and in the power of your divine Majesty to worship the Unity. . . .

So, by our Theme, we are invited and urged to move programmatically and intentionally to embrace the full Trinitarian text on which, for example, the Constitution of the World Council of Churches rests:

> The World Council of Churches is a fellowship of churches which confess the Lord Jesus Christ as God and Savior according to the Scriptures and therefore seek to fulfill together their common calling to the glory of the one God, Father, Son, and Holy Spirit.

To many Christians, especially in the West, it seems strange to think of God as somehow threesome and yet one. And they find it hard to believe the concept to be important. Or they leave it to theologians, because they feel it is without relevance for daily faith and life.

But I begin to see that my faith badly needs to be challenged by the Trinity, by the mystery that rescues me from picturing God in all too human form. It could be argued that no earlier period of the church has pictured God more as a "human" Father and

Jesus as a man than these last hundred years or so. Thereby the male-image of God became oppressive to many women, and by implication also to men. What a liberation to be reminded that it is equally true to speak of God as Spirit—and in Greek the Spirit is *it,* not he or He! As the theology of the church was articulated and written by men, this non-gender character of the Spirit was lost by assimilation within the masculine God language. Such an assimilation strikes many as inevitable, especially when the Latin term *persona,* with its original connotation of "role in a play," became the translation of what the Greeks called *hypostasis,* the term by which they expressed the concrete (substantive) manifestation of the one divine essence. But "person" spoke so much more directly to our need for a personal relation to God. And if the Spirit is a "person," then it seemed to require a personal pronoun.

In the church that turned out to be *He,* although in Hebrew the Spirit is *She,* as is

10

her sister Wisdom in both Hebrew and Greek *(Sophia)*.

I have come to experience the worship of the Triune God as a liberation from that spiritual or intellectual idolatry in which we picture God in our own image. To be sure, we can pray to God in the most intimate personal terms. But when we are in danger of letting our images of God harden into idols with our own racial or gender traits, the image changes into the "non-image" for spirit, and those who worship God must worship in spirit and truth (John 4:24).

So we learn to image God beyond our imaging and imagining, a mystery that is not in the image of splendid isolation but eternal being in mutual interrelationships, organic, cosmic, life-giving energy, creative and transcendent.

A prayer I learned long ago now takes on new meaning:

O thou eternal Wisdom, whom we partly know, and partly do not know;

O thou eternal Justice, whom we partly

acknowledge, but never wholly obey;
O thou eternal Love, whom we love a little,
but fear to love too much:
Open our minds that we may understand;
Work in our wills, that we may obey;
Kindle our hearts, that we may love thee. . . .

Is that a personal or an impersonal
prayer? When we pray so, that question
seems without meaning as our minds are
taught not to let our need for a personal
God tie down our imagination to human
forms in an idolatrous manner.

The Spirit is the indispensable vehicle to
take us towards a theology where our
images do not harden into mental idols.

As I write these pages, I shall teach my
soul and mind to say *It* about the Holy
Spirit. That way I will take seriously the
warning against picturing God in my own
image. The point can be made in many
ways. It is equally true to say about God
that she is black as it is to say he is white.
Or equally false. To meditate on God as
Spirit is an indispensable corrective.

# TWO

# The Theme is Right

As our story begins, in the very first verses of the Bible, the Spirit of God is sweeping as a wind over the dark waters of formless chaos. From that very first page the Spirit is the driving force, the creative energy, and the animating breath of the whole creation.

And when our story reaches its conclusion and completion on the last page of the Bible, to be sure, the Spirit is there: "The Spirit and the Bride (i.e., the church) say, 'Come.' And let those who hear say, 'Come.' And let those who desire take the water of life without price" (Rev. 22:17; cf. Isa. 55:1).

Our story is indeed permeated by the Spirit in thousands of ways through the whole Bible. We shall seek guidance, insight, and inspiration by being reminded of some of the gifts of the Spirit, gifts that promise energy and renewal for the whole Church, yea for the whole creation.

Before we look for the special gifts of the Spirit we should recognize that the theme *Come, Holy Spirit—Renew the Whole Creation* catches the very thrust of the biblical dynamism of the Spirit—from Creation to Redemption. The many theological debates about the nature of eschatology, the continuities and the discontinuities between nature and grace, the coming of the kingdom of heaven within or beyond the borders of history, etc., should not obscure the simple fact that God's story is one about the good creation, the damage done to it, and its mending. When Jesus chooses to make the kingdom of God the central theme of his ministry, he affirms in words and deeds that the aim of the exercise is the renewal of God's creation. And the glorious panorama of the new heaven and the new earth and of the Holy City with the trees of life—"and the leaves of the tree were for the healing of the nations . . ." (Rev. 22:2)—what else can that be about but the renewal of God's creation towards restored and sustainable life?

**A creation worth renewing**

Our theme suggests on good biblical authority that the creation is worth renewing, not only that it is in need of being renewed. Let us take hold of that insight. There have been periods in the history of the church when people liked to enhance the glory and significance of Jesus Christ by painting the created world as so depraved and human beings so deeply fallen that the affirmation of God's good and wise creation—if such an affirmation was made at all—had no operative power in the lives of Christians. That affirmation was at best a background against which the Fall became that much more definite in defining the human condition.

But we are well advised, not least if we experience God as Triune—Creator, Redeemer, and Inspiration—to give God full honor for the wise and good creation. The creation is worth our tender attention.

Of course we cannot know why God created the world. But we can and may speculate, provided we do not claim certainty for

15

our speculations. Such speculations are born out of love for and fascination with God. One could say that God could have avoided many worries and much pain by remaining in splendid isolation. But there seems to be something in the very heart of God, in God's very essence, that desires community, desires giving and receiving, desires communication. Eastern Orthodox piety and theology have plumbed some of the depths of the ever-giving and receiving interdependence among the Father and the Son and the Spirit. Perhaps there is more to be learned about God as love already in God's act of creation.

### The Sabbath

Scholars tell us that the creation story in the first chapter of Genesis presumably has a priestly origin. It is told from the perspective of the sanctity of the Sabbath. By its affirmation of God's resting on the seventh day it builds the principle of rest into the very structure of the cosmos. This powerful perspective gives us not only a legitimization of the Sabbath. It gives the day of rest a meaning that does not need to be motivated by the pragmatic argument that with rest on the Sabbath/Sunday we can work all the better during the week. Rest has a dignity all of its own.

The practice of "the Sabbath" and the rhythm of the seven-day week that follows from it are perhaps the most widespread and humanly beneficial contribution of Jewish Law, mediated through Christianity to the world community—the now almost globally practiced rhythm of weeks and weekends.

But in the Bible the sabbatical principle also informs the view of nature and the views of property. In the so-called Sabbath year (the seventh year) the land shall rest, lying fallow. In the Jubilee year (the fiftieth, following 7 x 7 years) the economic equilibrium is to be restored and mortgages paid, or forgiven in case the debtor cannot pay. Here the principle of the Sabbath is clearly shown to be a protection against unlimited striving and unrelenting drive for profit. Every fiftieth year is to break that spiral by which the rich are becoming richer and the poor are becoming poorer.

Scholars debate whether and to what extent these laws (in Lev. 25) were put into practice, and different historical periods have come up with different interpretations. But two things seem rather clear. (1) The principle of setting a limit to maximum work and a limit to maximum gain is part of the wise creation and not contrary to it. (2) The present debt crisis in the world makes this principle obviously and commandingly relevant: If payment cannot be made, the debt must be forgiven; otherwise the equilibrium of the creation is endangered.

## The beauty of creation

As one reads both the first and the last chapters of the Bible one is struck by their beauty and their harmony. The images of the garden of paradise and the city of the New Jerusalem have left indelible imprints on Christian imagination. If we take time to ponder God's wise and good creation, we

should pause long enough to let its beauty
sink in. For the beautiful, that which pleases
our eyes and all our senses, is worth our
admiration and gratitude. "And God saw
everything that he had made, and behold, it
was very good" (Gen. 1:31). Actually, the
capacity to be arrested by the beauty of God's
creation guards well against that itchy prag-
matism by which we manipulate nature
under the arrogant misconception that the
whole world exists just for us and for our use.
The sense of beauty helps us to experience the
sanctity of nature. Here lies the difference
between two kinds of ecological attitudes.
Some say: If we do not behave, we shall have
no clean air to breathe and no clean water to
drink. But others rather show their respect
for the integrity of creation by just enjoying
its beauty and tending it gently. A cultivation
of the sense of beauty is often thought of as a
luxury, since it cannot be argued on strictly
utilitarian grounds. But I think it is akin to
the sense of worship, praising God and enjoying God for ever.

## The *imago Dei*—in God's image

God created the human *(ha-adam)* in his own image, in the image of God he created him, male and female God created them (Gen. 1:27).

The Lord formed the human *(ha-adam)* of dust from the ground *(ha-adamah)* and breathed into his nostrils the breath of life, and man became a living being (Gen. 2:7).

By these two complementary verses the Bible defines what it is to be a human being. In Hebrew, Adam was not a name as it later became, but a designation: THE ADAM. In Greek it was rendered "human being" *(anthropos)*, rather than "man" *(aner)*. Around these two verses generations of believers and schools of scholars have woven interpretations and speculations. This is the starting point. When we human beings call on the Holy Spirit, this is where we should begin.

It is hard to imagine a bolder and more intense expression of human dignity than the image of God, the *imago Dei*, especially when we remember the Bible's aversion to any and all images of God. Of course, we notice the same wonderful effect of oscillation as we found in the imaging of the Triune God: As the mind fastens on "Adam" as a single figure, the image changes into the plural "male and female God created *them*." And when we hear "Adam" exclaim in another context about Eve: "This at last is bone of my bones and flesh of my flesh . . ." the point may well be likeness and equality—rather than the derivation and dependence, which male interpreters took for granted was the point.

In the second verse that we quoted above, human dignity is affirmed by God breathing the breath of life, God's Spirit (cf. Eccl. 12:7), into dust from the ground (the *adamah*).

What generosity on the part of God to make the *imago Dei* in such brittle and non-lasting material! What a treasure in earthen vessels, to use a famous quote from the apostle Paul (2 Cor. 4:7).

In recent dialogues with Muslims and Jews I have been struck by the persistence with which all three—Jews, Muslims, and Christians—seek themselves back to the creation of all human beings in the image of God, prior to any covenants and distinctions. Jewish tradition recalls the question and answer of the sages: Why did God create all human beings from one? So that no one should be able to say: "My father is greater than your father."

Jews, Muslims, and Christians—and in different forms many other religions—have this precious insight in their scriptures and traditions. But that insight has not always been fully operative. It has seemed more important to stress rather those elements of identity that give our traditions their specificity as Christians or as Jews or as Muslims. But as we grope for the resources of our faiths towards peace with justice and justice with peace, the time has come to return to basics. All human beings are created in the image of God, later covenants and revelations notwithstanding.

22

But what about the Fall? What about Genesis 3? In large parts of Christendom and during many periods, the teaching of the fall into human depravity has made the doctrine of the *imago Dei* a rather pointless ornament or a perspective that made the depravity even more guilt-laden. The restoration of the image of God and the mending of a damaged creation by the Spirit's power of renewal did not seem to express the faith adequately. Was there anything left sufficiently healthy to warrant mending and renewal? Such questions contributed to making inoperative the biblical witness to the dignity of our common humanity in the image of God.

Actually the story in Genesis 3 about the serpent, Eve, and Adam has a fascinating double edge. To be sure, it is the story of disobedience and of expulsion from a paradise of innocence (typically then and through the ages, the man blames it on the woman). But on another level it is the story of human beings becoming capable of moral reasoning and responsibility. The words of the serpent are both true and false, both deceptive and illuminating. The capacity of "knowing good and evil," of moral reasoning and responsibility, puts, tragically and gloriously, an end to innocence. It is as if this were the adolescence of humankind, the *Bar mitzvah*, the Confirmation into maturity of life and faith with personal and intentional responsibility.

In a world in which life was seen as governed by fate—much as we now often refer to heredity and circumstances—Christians read Genesis 3 as a witness to human freedom of choice and responsibility. To be sure, Adam and Eve had been disobedient, but in Jesus Christ there has come new power to stand up against temptation. After all, was not Jesus the one who had bruised the head of the serpent when he was stung by death on Calvary (Gen. 3:15)? In such a perspective the story of the expulsion from paradise did enhance human dignity and heighten the possibility of a renewed life in the image of God by the power of the Holy Spirit so richly dispensed since Pentecost.

## The whole creation

"When you send forth your Spirit they are created; and you renew the face of the earth" (Ps. 104:30).

In the liturgy and Bible readings of many churches this verse forms part of the celebration of Pentecost. That was how I learned to hear those words. I heard them together with the prophet Joel's promise of the day when God's Spirit will be poured out on all flesh so that "your sons and your daughters shall dream dreams and your young men shall see visions" (Joel 2:28/Acts 2:17). I thought about the renewal of the quality of spiritual life and of our witness to God's mighty acts. And I guess I was right. But only in a partial manner, and in a manner that fed my human pride.

For in Psalm 104 those words about God's Spirit as creating and renewing the face of the earth speak not just of human beings, but of all God's creatures big and small:

24. O Lord, how manifold are thy works!
    In wisdom hast thou made them all;

the earth is full of thy creatures.

25. Yonder is the sea, great and wide,
which teems with things innumerable,
living things both small and great.

26. There go the ships
and Leviathan which thou didst
form to sport in it.

27. These all look to thee,
to give them their food in due season.

28. When thou givest to them, they gather
it up; when thou openest thy hand,
they are filled with good things.

29. When thou hidest thy face, they are
dismayed; when thou takest away their
breath, they die and return to their dust.

30. When thou sendest forth thy Spirit, they
are created; and thou renewest the face of
the ground. . . .

To me this is now an important reminder that God's Spirit is the breath of life in the whole creation. We cannot speak about human dignity in such a manner that we set ourselves up against the rest of God's creation.

We are part of that whole creation, and God's Spirit is not confined to us human beings, to our life and breath.

In many churches the words in verses 27 and 28 have shaped a beloved grace before meals:

The eyes of all wait upon you, O Lord,
and you give them their food in due season.
You open your gracious hand,
satisfying all living things.

Such words should remind us of our continuity with the whole creation, a creation where some creatures just delight in life, like that creature of much speculation, the Leviathan sporting in the sea.

In some parts of Christendom the practice of saying grace at meals has fallen into disuse. As sometimes happens with such acts of piety, the practice was felt to deteriorate into mere formality, without a prayerful spirit. But as we invoke the Holy Spirit to renew the whole creation it may well be that the practice of giving thanks to God and asking God's blessing at meals will take on a new meaning and urgency. For food links us substantially with the whole creation. And at mealtime we become conscious of those who have less or nothing. Hence the prayer from the churches in South America: To those who have hunger, give bread; and to us who have bread, give the hunger for justice.

So in many ways the sense of solidarity with the whole creation may grow among us. Come to think about it, in the biblical story of the creation we human beings did not get a full day to ourselves, although that is how most people remember the text: On the sixth day God created Adam. But that was in the afternoon, after the siesta, so to speak. We had to share that day with "all the living creatures according to their kinds: cattle and creeping things and beasts of the earth according to their kinds" (Gen. 1:24). It is almost as if God said with a smile: One day they will find out their continuity with creation, perhaps when Darwin comes, or perhaps when the voices of native peoples are heard again in the assemblies of the churches. . . .

And so we have our common origin and status as creatures by God's creating and renewing Spirit. That defines our identity just as much as our being formed in the image of God. In that balance lies the solidarity with the whole creation. As there were two ways to express the human dignity—the *imago Dei* in chapter 1 and the breath of God in chapter 2—so there are two expressions in the creation stories to bring out the relation between human beings and the rest of the creation. In Genesis 1:28 they are to subdue the earth and have dominion over all living things. In Genesis 2:15 God puts the Adam in the garden to till it and to keep it. The Hebrew word for "keep" *(shamar)* expresses care and protection. This is the word used in the Aaronic blessing: "The Lord bless you and keep you . . ." (Num. 6:24). It is the word used in Cain's defensive response: "Am I my brother's keeper?" (Gen. 4:9).

I have the distinct impression that Christian theologians and preachers through the ages have chosen—perhaps unconsciously —to quote and lift up the dominion motif far more often than that of keeping and tending with tender care. One can ask why, and one can pursue the positive and the negative impact of those two perspectives through history. But it is in the balance between them that a sustainable future lies.

The critics of Christianity have found fault with us on both counts, depending on the conditions and situations they were concerned about. There are times and situations when the main criticism leveled against the churches is over their resistance to scientific and technological changes and potentialities. We are criticized in that context for not living up to our mandate of exercising dominion over the creation. In more recent years, when technology is not so sure that it can correct or harness the calamities it causes, that verse in Genesis 1:28 has been blamed for all the ecological evils of the world.

30

The two perspectives need to complement each other. In our present crisis it is worth remembering also how the theme of dominion warns us against a mindless and passive acceptance of everything that is, even if the raw and jarring overtones and connotations of that very word "dominion"—which different translations can hardly soften—call us to be constantly watchful as to its use and misuse.

Perhaps the words of Jesus about those who lord it over their underlings have meaning also in the realm of human attitudes towards nature:

> You know that those who are supposed to rule over the nations lord it over them, and their great men exercise authority over them. But it shall not be so among you; but whoever would be great among you must be a servant, and whoever would be first among you must be slave of all. For the Son of Man also came not to be served but to serve and to give his life a ransom for many (Mark 10:42–45).

## God's Spirit in the ordinary and in the extraordinary

The one and the same Spirit of God sustains and permeates all life, all living things, according to their kinds. "When thou sendest forth thy Spirit they are created . . ." (Ps. 104:30). The Spirit gives life and shape. "The Spirit of God has made me, and the breath of the Almighty gives me life. . . . Behold I am towards God as you are; I too was formed from a piece of clay." Those are the words of Job's young friend Elihu who, a little earlier, had reminded Job that wisdom is not confined to old age, "but it is the Spirit in the person, the breath of the Almighty, that makes a person understand" (33:4, 6; 32:8).

The familiar words from Psalm 51 express beautifully how the Holy Spirit shapes, restores, and energizes our life, enlivening our own spirit:

> Create in me a clean heart, O God,
> and put a new and right spirit within me.
>
> Cast me not away from thy presence
> and take not thy holy Spirit from me.

Restore unto me the joy of thy salvation
and uphold me with a willing spirit (10–12).

So God's Holy Spirit is the life-giving center from which life, will, and emotions are cleansed and renewed.

That very same Spirit of God is also the Spirit behind artistic creativity, as God said to Moses about Bezalel who was to make the furnishings of the ark and the tent: "I have filled him with the Spirit of God, with ability and intelligence, with knowledge and all craftsmanship, to devise artistic designs . . ." (Ex. 31:2).

I find that aspect important for it is not only nature that has great beauty but also art and architecture. A Swedish poet once wrote: "I would like to carve a wooden spoon so plain that people see God . . ." (Karin Boye).

We know that same Spirit of God from the prophecy of Isaiah about the characteristics of the Messianic ruler:

And the Spirit of the Lord shall rest upon him, the spirit of wisdom and understanding, the spirit of counsel and might, the spirit of knowledge and the fear of the Lord . . . (Isa. 11:2).

And the prophecy goes on by painting the renewal of the creation in justice and with peace not only among people but between human beings and animals and between the wild and the tame: "And the calf and the lion shall feed together, with a little child to herd them" (v. 6).

It is the Spirit of the Lord that "came mightily upon David" when he was anointed by Samuel. It is the Spirit of the Lord that leaves Saul so that now David must soothe Saul's mental strain by playing his lyre. "David took his lyre and played it with his hand; so Saul was refreshed and was well . . ." (1 Sam. 16:13–23).

In a far more benign succession, the Spirit of the Lord that was in the prophet Elijah was seen to rest on his pupil Elisha when the chariot had taken Elijah out of Elisha's sight (2 Kings 2:12–18). And it comes as no surprise to us that one of the designations for a prophet is "a man of the Spirit" (Hos. 9:7) just as it is "a man of God" (e.g. 1 Sam. 9:6). As to the word "man," it is worth remembering that—no doubt due to the non-discriminatory nature of the Holy Spirit—it is exactly among the prophets that we also find women, such as Deborah (Judges 4). Like the other early prophets in Israel she is both a judge and prophet, and by the power of Spirit she shatters not only the enemies but also legions of stereotypes about the role of women through much of both biblical and post-biblical times.

As I think of how it is that one and the same Spirit of God energizes prophets and inspires beauty, I am reminded of how some languages (including English) use the word "grace," a word so important for understanding the nature of God and the possibilities of life. Think, for example, of the saying of one of the sixteenth-century English divines when he saw people condemned on the way to the gallows: "But for the *grace* of God, there go I." But we also speak of things being *graceful*

35

when they please our senses. So life is of one piece after all, for it all comes from God's Holy Spirit. Beauty and forgiveness are cousins in the family of the Holy Spirit.

To me such a hasty and telegraphic survey of some ways our Bible speaks of the Spirit of God becomes a mighty reminder of how the one and the same Holy Spirit gives life to nature and revelation to the prophets; the one and the self-same Holy Spirit radiates from the pages of holy writ and permeates my body and my heart of flesh, not of stone. So it makes much sense indeed to pray:

Come, Holy Spirit—Renew Your Whole
    Creation:
nature and grace,
soul and body,
economy and ecology,
matter hard and soft.
For you do renew the face of the whole earth,
of the whole cosmos
over which you moved
at the dawn of creation
as it was in the beginning, is now,
and shall be, world without end.

# THREE

# The Spirit of the Lord is Upon Me...

### The descent of the dove and the Spirit that was in Jesus

The life and ministry of Jesus is seen by all the evangelists as permeated by the Spirit. This is expressed in many ways and at different points in the ongoing story, and the Spirit is the energy by which his mighty deeds are wrought.

All four Gospels begin the ministry of Jesus with the same story: the baptism in the Jordan where the Holy Spirit descends on Jesus in the likeness of a dove (Mark 1:8–11; Matt. 3:13–17; Luke 3:21–22; John 1:29–34). The endearing symbol of the dove with its proverbial gentleness (Matt. 10:16) makes a Jewish *Targum* (the Aramaic translation of the Hebrew) render "the voice of the turtle-dove" in the Song of Songs (2:12) as the "voice of the Holy Spirit of redemption." In more recent times the dove has become the powerfully powerless symbol of peace, especially when the dove has the olive branch in her beak. That reminds us of the story of Noah where the dove brings the good tidings of having found dry land after the flood— which the more warlike raven did not. So the world has new hope for life, the catastrophe was not final, and God enters into a covenant with the creation not to destroy it. And the rainbow is the sign for that unconditional promise (Gen. 8–9). When we read that story in a nuclear age we are haunted by the afterthought: God has promised it all right and that unconditionally—but did the writer of the holy text ever fathom that human beings could themselves trigger global destruction?

For the evangelists the gentle dove represents the Spirit as "descending and remaining" over Jesus as the Spirit had hovered over the waters at creation (Gen. 1), and as the Presence of God rests on whatever is holy. Thus Jesus is empowered to baptize with the

Holy Spirit as he is authorized and pro-
claimed as the Son of God. The Gospel of
John brings it all together:

> And John [the Baptist] bore witness, "I
> saw the Spirit descend as a dove from
> heaven, and it remained on him. I myself
> did not know him; but he who sent me to
> baptize with water said to me, 'He on whom
> you see the Spirit descend and remain, this is
> he who baptizes with the Holy Spirit.' And I
> have seen and have borne witness that this is
> the Son of God" (1:32–34).

And Luke has a surprising and beautiful
way of taking the ancestry of Jesus beyond
Abraham (where Matthew stops) all the
way back to God, not only to Adam: ". . .
Seth (son) of Adam (son) of God." He links
the genealogy to the descent of the Spirit at
the baptism of Jesus (Luke 3:23–38)—not to
the Christmas story as does Matthew—thus
affirming that Jesus is "the Son of God."

In Matthew's and Luke's Gospels the
story begins at the birth of Jesus as a miracle

of the Holy Spirit. It is especially in Luke's tender image of the Virgin Mary that divinity and humanity are brought together by a mystery in which the *imago Dei* is restored: human existence in the image of God. Or with the words from the Epistle to the Colossians: "For in Christ the whole fullness of divinity dwells bodily . . ." (2:9).

"In the beginning was the Word" (the Logos; with the further connotation of structuring power, and reason) . . . "and the Word became flesh . . ." is how John says it. Just as the Spirit was with God at creation, so also was that mighty and clear Word—and Wisdom sophia, the sister of the Word. Such thoughts of loving reflection among interpreters of the holy texts intensify the link between the beginning in creation and the recreative breakthrough in Jesus Christ as the Son of God, made known as such when the Holy Spirit descends and rests on him.

The three synoptic Gospels (i.e., Matthew, Mark, and Luke) want us to remember that the first event in the life of Jesus once he was under the sway of the Spirit was his time of testing by the temptations in the wilderness.

Actually they all say that it was by that very Spirit of God that he was placed that arid and devastated place among the wild and unfriendly beasts. This is the reverse image of paradise. The writers and readers of the Gospels no doubt saw Jesus passing the test as a sign that it was now possible in the power of the Holy Spirit to stand up against the assault of Satan and to be ministered to by God's good angels. The reversal of the expulsion from paradise is in the making. One comes to think of Jesus' words to the criminal at his side at Golgotha: "Today you shall be with me in paradise" (Luke 23:43).

And so Jesus returned to Galilee, as Luke puts it, "in the power of the Spirit," and then Luke sees the whole ministry of Jesus through the prism of the words of the prophet Isaiah read that day in his home synagogue:

The Spirit of the Lord is upon me because he has anointed me to preach good news to the poor. He has sent me to

41

proclaim release to the captives and recovering of sight to the blind, to set at liberty those who are oppressed, to proclaim the welcome year of the Lord (Luke 4:18–19/Isa. 61:1–2a).

Energized and authenticated by the Spirit, Jesus' ministry will be one of liberation, healing, and justice. It will be a ministry where words and actions are woven into one. By the power of the Spirit persons are healed and relationships mended. We often feel that his words are mainly commentaries on and illustrations of his acts of healing and restoring life. It is surprising—and striking—that not a single passage in the synoptic Gospels refers to the Holy Spirit as the source or authenticator of the *words* of Jesus. The Spirit engenders *action*. The Spirit of the Lord rests upon him and works through him nothing less than a renewal of creation.

In the language of the Gospels, the term for that renewal is the kingdom of God/of heaven. (In spite of all its difficult associations with kings and other male potentates of this world, I prefer the word "kingdom" to "realm" or "reign" or "dominion," for it does have a concrete and social dimension, with people and communities restored. To me that rescues the word, "kingdom," for our use, redeeming it from being just an expression of power.) And, as we have seen already, this deliberate choice by Jesus is the clearest sign that his ministry is to be seen as the crucial act in the great biblical drama of God's ever ongoing struggle for the mending of the creation by the work of the Spirit.

### Blasphemy against the Holy Spirit

Hence all attempts at discrediting this mending of the creation are judged most harshly. In a story found in Mark 3:22–30 we hear about those who accuse Jesus of satanic magic. It is such perverse unwillingness to rejoice in the healing and restoring power of the Spirit that is branded as blasphemy against the Holy Spirit—the sin beyond forgiveness (Mark 3:29–30).

That verse from the Gospels belongs to those words that have caused much consternation and pain through the history of the church. As we invoke the Holy Spirit to renew the whole creation, we may well have a vantage point from which to understand better this harsh word of Jesus.

For it seems that the issue is an ever-recurring tendency among the establishments and the guardians of faith and order both in church and society. I am conscious of that tendency in myself. Instead of asking first of all whether something has the marks of enhancing life and justice, peace and well-being, I tend to look at the credentials or the party, or the theology or the ideology, or the morality or the pedigrees or academic degrees or whatever of those who offer their labor in their various callings. But according to the irrefutable words of Jesus it is by the fruit that a tree is to be judged. And revealing indeed is the story about the disciples telling Jesus how they had come across someone who performed miracles in Jesus' name "but does not follow us." Proudly they tell Jesus that they forbade him to do so. To which Jesus says: Don't! Then he enunciates the proverbial wisdom: "The one who is not against us is for us" (Mark 9:38–40). All of which provides a critique of that possessive and apologetic attitude that is contrary to the spirit of generosity and to the generosity of God's Spirit. We are reminded of the word of the employer to the more established work force that was critical of him when he did not pay according to hours of work, only according to human needs: "Why do you look with greedy eyes at my generosity?" (Matt. 20:15).

It all adds up to this: If the aim of the exercise, the goal of God, is the mending of the creation, then it is the blasphemy of blasphemies to think that only what is done in the church, by the church, and through the church—and/or by and through Christians—can be of God and all else is wrong and destructive. When we are so driven by defensiveness on God's—or even more on Christ's—behalf we are in danger of the blasphemy against the Holy Spirit. Then we are at cross purposes with our prayer: *Come, Holy Spirit—Renew the Whole Creation.*

In fact one of the few passages in the Old Testament (Ps. 51:11 is another) that uses the term "Holy Spirit" (instead of the Spirit of God, the Spirit of the Lord, etc.) speaks of ways in which a people rebelling against God's generous goodness and steadfast love has *grieved* God's Holy Spirit—that Holy Spirit that God had put in the midst of the people, that Spirit of the Lord that gave the people rest (Isa. 63:10). As the power of renewal intensifies in the ministry of Jesus, so does causing grief to the Holy Spirit sharpen into blasphemy. But valid remains Isaiah's ensuing cry of prayer: "We have become like those over whom thou hast never ruled, like those who are not called by thy name. O that thou wouldst rend the heavens and come down . . ." (Isa. 63:19–64:1).

**Birth and growth of life**

The Gospel of John enriches our faith by giving us its own quite distinct understanding of Jesus' life and ministry. The other Gospels write and think in metaphors drawn from the social and political life (kingdom, justice, servants, masters, etc.); the Gospel of John uses a language of the life sciences, speaking much of birth and life and growth, and of branches remaining, abiding in the tree to be enlivened by the sap. Thus Jesus came that we should have life, and that abundantly (10:10). In John it is all about life, the processes of life. From the beginning was the Word, the Logos . . . and it was life, and the life was the light of humanity (1:1 and 4). And so John speaks of the Spirit giving birth to a new life of divine quality (the Greek word *anothen* in John 3:3 can mean both born "anew" and born "from above"). For John faith is really to live by this stream of life. "Those who believe in me . . . out of their hearts shall flow rivers of living water. Now this he said about the Spirit which those who believed in him were about to receive . . ." (7:38–39). The life of faith is the eternal life; it is a life called eternal since it is in communion and continuity with the Eternal One. To John "eternal" does not refer to quantity of time, but to quality of life. "Truly, truly I say to you, those who hear my word and believe God who sent me, have eternal life and do not come into judgment, but have passed from death to life" (5:24, cf. 11:25–26).

Thus it is all about life, the life reborn by the Spirit. I belong to a church that believes it right to baptize infants, and part of the liturgy stresses the need for a new birth. It seems odd, considering that the baby has just been born a few days or weeks before. Precisely for that reason I have had to reflect on the Johannine birth-language by which a new birth is seen as reinforcing and revitalizing life on the model of the creation itself, that is, when God breathed breath/spirit into earthy matter. "That which is born of the flesh is flesh, and that which is born of the Spirit, spirit" (John 3:6). In the culture in which I live, I have come to feel strongly that when the little child is baptized, it is set free from all the social shackles of class and race and gender and even, somehow, the genetic chains of causality. Born anew in the Spirit in holy baptism, the child is restored into the freshness of the day of creation, now pulsating with a life of divine quality. And if this liberation from all that binds and hampers the fullness of life is true about a baby, imagine the grace of baptism in later years when life has become so much more entangled in circumstances both of our own making and of our surroundings.

It is all about life, a life mirrored in the divine life of the Holy Trinity, of which the Gospel of John writes with such insight. Especially when the Gospel grounds the oneness of the church not in divine or authoritarian principles that rule the world but using that "biological" language of being interwoven in an abiding manner: ". . . that they may all be one, even as thou, Father, art in me, and I in thee, that also they may be in us . . ." (17:21). As I read and meditate on such words I almost see the flow of the life-giving Spirit through the arteries and the veins of God's creation. And the flow of that energy is perfectly unobstructed. And what we call sin and disobedience become the obstruction and the hardening of the arteries —impeding the flow of the Holy Spirit, the life-blood of abundant life.

Before we leave the rich and deeply benefi-cial insights of the Johannine perspective and its language of life, we must also remember that John does not use words that refer to death and dying when he speaks of the cruci-fixion. It is as if his sharp focus on LIFE makes him shy away from such words. Rather, Jesus is "lifted up," both in analogy to how Moses lifted up the serpent in the wilder-ness for the healing of the people (3:14), and in cosmic exaltation, "when I am lifted up from the earth, I shall draw all things unto myself" (12:32). To John the death of Jesus is his glory, ". . . the time has come for the Son of Man to be glorified" (12:23). And so, to John's memory and understanding, the final word of Jesus as he is lifted up on the cross is one of victory, even triumph. "It is accomplished" (19:30). Then the sentence by which John concludes this part of the story can be translated: "And bowing his head he *handed over* the Spirit" . . . back to God or on to the church. For John, Jesus does not breathe his last, he does not just yield up his spirit. He actively hands over the Spirit, the Spirit that he had promised would guide the disciples in days to come, the Spirit that had descended and remained over him as his ministry began. Had he not said: ". . . It is to your advantage that I go away, for if I do not go away, the Counselor [the Spirit] will not come to you . . ." (16:7)?

## The defense attorney

There is another lesson about the work of the Spirit to be learned from the Gospels. Recorded by the synoptic evangelists is only one situation in which the disciples are assured of the special assistance of the Holy Spirit, and that is when they are dragged before the authorities, be they religious or secular. Then they need not worry in advance about what to say, for it will be given to them by the Spirit, "for it is not you who speak but the Holy Spirit" (Mark 13:11, cf. Luke 12:11–12, Matt. 10:18–20).

In the Gospel of John the Holy Spirit is called by a title that can have many meanings and connotations: *Parakletos* (John 14:16, 26, 15:26, 16:7, cf. about Jesus in 1 John 2:1). The translators choose different words: Comforter (KJV, The Living Bible, so also Luther); Counselor (NIV, RSV); "the one who is coming to stand by you" (Phillips); advocate (NEB); Advocate (NRSV); Helper (New American Standard and as an alternative in NRSV). Even when the word is given the more general sense of Comforter or even Helper, the connotation of Advocate, counsel for the defense, should not be lost, especially in the light of the assurance of the Spirit's assistance when a disciple of Jesus is taken to law courts or faces other authorities.

Which all goes a long way to warn us against thinking of the Spirit primarily as comfort for the already comfortable, or as belonging primarily to the realm of warm religious experiences of grace and forgiveness.

It seems that one indispensable function of the Spirit is to make our witness for Christ and the kingdom of justice and peace on earth bold enough to confront and rattle the powers that be. Then it feels good to have an able defense lawyer with you, especially for those who cannot afford the services of the legal profession.

# FOUR

# In Fellowship with the Holy Spirit

Most Bible readers would have noticed that the frequent references to the kingdom that characterize the Gospels of Matthew, Mark, and Luke are not found in the Epistles or in the Acts of the Apostles. This is the more striking when we read the Acts of the Apostles. For here it is the same writer who holds the pen—or dictates the words. Luke seems to be aware of this difference between Jesus' language and the language of the church. He actually makes of it a programmatic point.

Because the kingdom was the central theme in the teaching and preaching of Jesus, the Book of Acts begins at that point. Also the risen Lord "was speaking of the kingdom of God" during those forty days before the Ascension (1:3). Thus it is only natural that the disciples should ask if the time has come for "restoring the kingdom." Jesus answers that God's timing is not for human knowing or calculation. "BUT you shall receive power when the Holy Spirit has come upon you, and you shall be my witnesses in Jerusalem and Judea and Samaria and to the end of the earth" (1:8).

### The Acts of the Holy Spirit

Luke has a great sense of symmetry, and his traditions are organized in orderly patterns of time and space. The ministry of Jesus began with the descending of the Spirit, and so Jesus progresses from the provinces to the city of Jerusalem. Now the life of the church begins in Jerusalem, in the Temple, with the descending of the Spirit on the disciples, and in the power of that Spirit they will bear witness in words and actions and through martyrdom (the Greek word for "witness") far beyond the lands traversed by Jesus. The Book of Acts itself brings the witness all the way to Rome, the capital of the world that Luke knew.

Now the Spirit is the energy and the guide engineering the life and expansion of the church in the world of the Jewish diaspora and through it to the Gentile world. The ecstatic speech, the speaking in tongues, of which we also know from Paul (Rom. 8:26; 1 Cor. 12–14), is seen by Luke as a symbol of the global outreach across all barriers of language and culture (Acts 2:5–13).

The Acts of the Apostles could just as well, or even better, be called "the Acts of the Holy Spirit," and there are indeed few chapters in the book without specific references to such acts. Here are a few examples. Beyond the breakthrough experiences of Pentecost in chapter 2 there is the power of healing in chapter 3. We see a community with its boldness of speech and willingness to share with one another all their belongings (chapter 4). Hence the gruesome story about Ananias and Sapphira. When they lied to the church about their wealth, they actually lied to the Holy Spirit (5:3) and to God. "You have not lied to people but to God" (5:4).

Peter's decisive move to full acceptance of Gentiles comes not until the Holy Spirit descends on Cornelius and his people (10:44–47). When the ensuing theological controversies are settled in the so-called Apostolic Council in Jerusalem, a letter is sent out to the churches in which the decision is presented with the words: "For it has seemed good to the Holy Spirit and to us . . ." (15:28). Also Paul's itinerary is led by the Spirit, as it tells him what he can expect (20:23) or as it hinders him from following his own plans (16:6; cf. Paul's own, less benign understanding of the same event in 1 Thess. 2:18, ". . . but Satan hindered us"). And at the very end of the book it is the Holy Spirit that had foreseen that the expansion of the church would be in the Gentile world to which the apostles bear witness (28:25–28).

## No nostalgia

So the stage is set for the first decades, and for all times in the community of those devoted to Jesus Christ. It is striking that the followers of Jesus did not dream themselves back to the time when he had walked with them and talked with them. It is astonishing how small a role the words of Jesus, which were later made part of our Gospels, play in the early Christian writings, the letters of Paul and of others, and even in Luke's account of the first decades of the church. In Luke's case we know that he knew that material since he had written his "first book," his Gospel, after careful research (Luke 1:1–4).

So they did not look back in nostalgia. They looked forward and they lived power-fully in the *now* of the Holy Spirit. One really feels the truth of Jesus' words of farewell in the Gospel of John: "I tell you the truth: It is to your advantage that I go away, for if I do not go away, the Counselor will not come to you, but if I go, I'll send him to you . . . I have yet many things to say to you, but you cannot bear them now. When the Spirit of truth comes, it will guide you into all the truth . . ." (16:7 ff).

Thus, when we pray: *Come, Holy Spirit,* our prayer is well in keeping with the mode and mood of faith which was tried and tested as the church began to understand itself, its promises, and its identity.

## Koinonia

As one reads about those first Christians one is inclined to exclaim: What a fellowship, what a *koinonia*, it must have been! I am sure it was, as they "devoted themselves to the apostles' teaching and the fellowship, to the breaking of the bread and the prayers" (Acts 2:42). At least in contemporary American Christianity the word "fellowship" has gained great popularity—quite a number have even picked up the Greek word *koinonia* as a powerful designation for community spirit. Some people even make it into a verb, "to fellowship" (churches are often evaluated by the warmth and friendliness by which people "fellowship together"). In such a cultural setting it may be refreshing or even necessary to remember that *koinonia* means a participation in something, and it is that something that produces community—sometimes even the feeling of community. But the community and the sense of community are by-products, caused by that something. Paul ends his second letter to the church in Corinth with the blessing that has become one of the most beloved and most often used: "The grace of the Lord Jesus Christ, and the love of God, and the fellowship of the Holy Spirit be with you all" (2 Cor. 13:13). There you have it: the *koinonia*, the participation, the sharing in the Holy Spirit. Paul had written earlier to them about the *koinonia*, the participation in the body and blood of Christ, in the blessing of the cup and the breaking of the bread (1 Cor. 10:16).

So strong was this understanding that faith was to have a part in the Holy Spirit that the ancient translators (Latin, Coptic, and Syriac, for example) interpreted the *koinonia* in Acts 2:42 as referring to the participation in the breaking of the bread, not as a fellowship that was something in itself: "the apostolic teaching, the participation in the eucharist and the prayers."

I believe that we have here a sobering reminder and an important warning. It can help us to see that the church does not become a club of like-minded, like-looking, like-acting, like-feeling people who experience an ever warmer fellowship the more like one another they are. In fellowship with the Spirit there is no such comfort for the comfortable. Paul learned that truth in a special way in Corinth.

## Paul's ecumenical breakthrough

It was the situation in Corinth that drove the apostle Paul to see and articulate how the Holy Spirit makes it possible and necessary for the church to handle diversity in a creative manner. In places where his authority was recognized, as seems to have been the case in Galatia, Paul tends to lay down the rules, expecting to be obeyed. His language is harsh, and it is clear that he expects to be obeyed (Gal. 1:9). But in the Corinthian church Paul seems to have had less influence. In any case, his tone is quite different. In writing to Christians in Corinth he explains his understanding of the diversity of the gifts that come from the one Spirit, the diverse members and the one Body (1 Cor. 12). Here and in chapter 3 Paul comes to an ecumenical view of the various fashions, factions, and schools of teaching in the church. The secular way—Paul calls it a "carnal, fleshly" way (1 Cor. 3:1–3)—is to look at diverse teachings as people look at different schools of philosophy and ideology, often named after their teachers, be they Paul or Apollos, Plato or Aristotle, Luther or Marx. But that paradigm does not apply to the church. Here the right paradigms are God's garden and God's building project where we are co-workers, all to be saved even if we did not build so well (v. 15). Or we are God's temple and the Spirit of God dwells in us. So the secular models do not apply. We can afford to withhold judgment of one another's teaching, leaving the judgment to God, to be pronounced in God's good time (4:5).

As I try to picture Paul's liberating "paradigms of the Spirit" in 1 Cor. 3–4, I find many of my own ideas of ecumenism far too timid and far too secular. Paul's is a model when he is, as usual, quite convinced that he is right, that he builds with good and lasting material—but that does not settle the matter. That would be a secular, not a spiritual way of thinking. "I am not aware of being wrong, but that does not make me right; it is God who judges me" in matters of my theology, so let us work side by side without partisanship (4:4 ff).

### Diversity and unity in the Spirit

But it is in his reflections on the various gifts of the Spirit that Paul works out most fully that insight of his about the diversity and unity in the one Spirit. Apparently the church in Corinth experienced great tensions, and especially the more spectacular manifestations of the Spirit such as glossolalia (speaking in tongues) caused some to feel more spiritual than others—with many analogies through the history of the church. Paul's corrective is clear and simple: "Now there are varieties of gifts, but the same *Spirit,* varieties of service, but the same *Lord,* varieties of actions, but the same *God* who activates it all in everyone. To each is given a manifestation of the Spirit for the common good" (12:4–7).

This variety in the oneness of the Trinity (Spirit, Lord, God) is then demonstrated and supported by the beautiful image of the one body and the many members. In Paul's Hellenistic world this was a well-known metaphor in popular philosophical teaching about society. But to make sure that the image is used with full mutuality and inter-dependence between the members of the community, Paul here brings in that famous poem of his in praise of love (1 Cor. 13). It is good to remember that its function, its address, that which gives the words the highest density of meaning, is exactly to show a way—the "still more excellent way" (12:31)—of oneness in the Spirit and richness in diversity.

### Love is to esteem the other

Paul uses the word for love *(agape)* that the Jewish translators of the Hebrew scriptures into Greek had found most appropriate, a word which had the connotation of "esteem." And he teaches us that love is measured by its elasticity, its capacity not to be irritated by that which is different and not to insist on one's own way. This is not just tolerance, but a positive embracing of the other in the awareness that it is those who have different gifts and visions who can enrich me and our common community.

Sometimes the theological agenda of some traditions has made *agape* into a catchword for God's unmotivated love of the undeserving sinner—as if God said: So great is my love that I can love even a wretch like you! But such "love" does not lift up, does not restore. For it is tainted by condescension. It is not *agape*. God's love as manifested so clearly in Jesus Christ is rather the capacity to discern that which is lovable where the world often does not. Jesus loved sinners. He did not just make them objects of love. He saw something he liked in them. That is why their human dignity was restored.

The word *agape* retains that same tone of "esteem" when Paul uses it as the key to ecumenism. It refers to the capacity of welcoming that which is different from one's own in the happy expectation of enrichment both of community and self. Here it becomes important how one renders the Greek in one of the lines of Paul's ode to *agape*. The trend has been to say that love is "not selfish" or "not self-seeking," but the King James Version got it right by its more literal translation of the Greek *ou zetei ta heautes* by ". . . seeketh not her own." For the point is that *agape* is hungry for the Other, for diversity. Moralizing words like "selfish" and "self-seeking" do not make that clear enough, and even RSV's "does not insist on its own way" hardly expresses the active reaching out toward that which is different, which is the hallmark of true *agape*.

Only with the elasticity of such *agape*, such esteem of the other, can the community flourish. That is why love is said to be even greater than faith and hope (13:13). In the same spirit, we read in Colossians 3:14 that love is like a belt that holds together the flowing robe of all good qualities and virtues—lest we trip on it. So without love, even faith and hope can go wrong.

Secular patterns of thought, even if applied to matters of faith and order, are restricted by so-called zero-sum thinking, i.e., my gain is the other's loss and vice versa. But in the Spirit there is no such scarcity imposed on us.

### The Spirit and the mind

When Paul at a later time writes to Rome, he goes over some of the material he has dealt with in his letter to the Corinthians. He once again makes use of the metaphor of the body and its members, in order to show how differences in gifts should be understood. But now he chooses to highlight the mind, the way one thinks, and not the Holy Spirit. The models of his thought in Romans 12 are, however, the same as in the Spirit chapters of Corinthians. But he plays in another key. (Some translations make that difference less clear by translating *logike latreia* by "spiritual worship" [12:1], but Paul is no doubt referring to that worship that is right for us as rational beings; KJV's "your reasonable service" meant just that in 1611. If we wanted to make it quite clear, we could translate the expression as "your intellectual worship."

In Romans 12 it is all about how rational beings can be transformed and serve God, "transformed by the renewal of your mind, so that you can discern what is the will of God, what is good, acceptable, and perfect" (12:1–2). And it is all about how to *think* (vv. 3, 16–18). Paul's switch from the Holy Spirit to the mind in dealing with the same issues suggests to me that we should not play the Spirit against the intellect or the intellect against the Spirit. The image that emerges when we place 1 Corinthians 12 and Romans 12 side by side is that of a mind enlivened by faith—and a faith kept crisp by the mind. The church has suffered much by the attempts at pitting mind against spirit, theology against spirituality, reason against faith—indeed, by all schizophrenic attempts at dividing mind and spirit.

I hope that I do not say this only because I have been a professor during most of my ministry. The issue is more serious than that. It has struck me again and again how much evil in this world is due to the ways we think. Our wills, our intentions, and our feelings are often pretty decent. No great evil is accomplished by invitations to be evil. Evil is not that popular. As the apostle says: "Satan disguises himself as an angel of light" (2 Cor. 11:14). It is often our ways of thinking that trip us up, that hold us back in that "confor-

70

mity to this world" of which Paul spoke as being much in need of transformation.

It is not so much in our hearts as it is in our habits of thinking that all those distortions of our humanity fester. It is in the inertia of our minds that they linger: racism, consumerism, classism, sexism, and all the other preconceptions by which our thinking is held captive.

I wonder if that was what Paul thought about, perhaps unconsciously, when he switched from the emotional intensities of the Corinthian tensions to his image of Rome with its power centers that set the stage and designed the rules for the whole empire. Perhaps that is how it happened that Paul came to put his stress on the renewal of *thinking*.

We have learned in recent years the necessity of "consciousness-raising." That is how one wakes up from conformity, and the transformation begins towards the renewal of the mind. Come to think of it, the Greek word for the "repentance" to which Jesus called his listeners *(metanoia)* actually refers to the mind, to a change of consciousness *(nous/noia);* and *meta* often has the connotation of raising to a higher level.

### The Spirit of glory and the solidarity with creation

At times Paul describes the Christian life as one where the Spirit of God or Christ functions as the breath of life, thus restoring life. "If the Spirit of him who raised Jesus from the dead dwells in you, he who raised Christ Jesus from the dead will give life to your mortal bodies also, through his Spirit which dwells in you" (Rom. 8:11). Or, in another context more related to our knowledge of God: "For what person knows her thoughts except the spirit which is in her? So also no one comprehends the thoughts of God except the Spirit of God. Now we have received . . . the Spirit which is from God . . ." (2:11); or as he says in the last words of that chapter: "We have the mind of Christ" (2:16).

But it is as if Paul was afraid of his own words. He is capable, by the inner logic of his faith and his theology, to make these boldest of statements as to how the Spirit transforms and enlightens, recreates and liberates. Even so, he always feels the need to warn against any overstatement of our salvation. The eighth chapter of his letter to the Romans gives striking examples of both sides of his thinking. It goes from sublime statements of bliss and glory to heavy reminders of how we must live in solidarity with the whole creation, which is groaning in travail until now. We know in new and terrible ways how true that is. So, even if we have what Paul calls the first fruits of the Spirit, we live only in faith, in expectation. Our redemption is as much in the future for us as for the rest of the world. Paul is afraid of any piety, any spirituality that has lost its solidarity with the whole creation.

Paul knows that it can be pretty depressing to face squarely the futility and the decay and all that impedes and mocks what

he calls "the glorious liberty of the children
of God" (v. 21). He knows a lot about
weakness and helplessness, partly perhaps
from that illness that seems at times to have
made him unable to do what he wanted to
do for the Lord (cf. 2 Cor. 12:7–10 and 4:7,
Gal. 4:13). He knows about times when he
did not have enough energy or sense of
direction to pray a decent prayer. At such
times, he says, the Spirit intercedes for us
with wordless sighs that God knows and
understands (8:26).

### Advice rather than commandment

Actually, Paul comes to an understanding
of the Holy Spirit out of his weakness and
his bewilderment. I think especially of his
answers to all the questions the Corinthians
seem to have asked him about sex and mar-
riage and celibacy (1 Cor. 7). On some he
has clear commandments to fall back on (v.
10). But on some there are no such ("I say,
not the Lord . . .", v. 12). So he gives them his
advice, pointing out that it is only that, not a

word from the Lord ("I think . . .," v. 26). And he ends by saying: "I *think* that also I have the Spirit of God" (v. 40). He think so, he does not know for sure.

To me, there are two important lessons about the Spirit in that attitude of Paul's. The first is that we need to invoke the Spirit when we do *not* know, when we are uncertain, when new situations present themselves. Both historians and theologians have difficulties admitting that there are new questions, not only variations of old ones. Paul may have been the last preacher in Christendom who dared to admit that there was no command of the Lord to answer some of the questions at hand. It is in such situations that we need to invoke the Spirit (cf. the words cited earlier from John 16:12 ff). Most often we tend to "use" the Spirit rather to guarantee and defend the already well defined.

The other lesson to learn from Paul is to keep the distinction clear between advice and commandment. Both the church and individual Christians have a tendency to claim the authority of God and the Holy Spirit for more of our words and views and opinions than is warranted. Paul had the honesty and the humility to make a clear distinction between advice and command-ment, hoping that his advice too was of the Spirit but not claiming for it infallible authority. Not least in our time of radically new issues (e.g., of genetics) or drastically new understandings of old issues (e.g., homosexuality), it may well be that the advisory mode, sensitive to the Spirit, is the proper one for our churches.

## The *imago Dei* —the emerging image of God

We have seen and heard about many ways in which Christians experienced and pictured the work, the energy, the wisdom and the gifts of the Spirit. Perhaps one of the most powerful articulations comes at a cru-cial point in Paul's reflection about his min-istry as a ministry of a renewed covenant, not a covenant of the dead letter but of the life-giving Spirit (2 Cor. 3). His reflections end with the stunning words:

> And we all, with unveiled faces, beholding the glory of the Lord, are being changed into that same image from glory to glory; for this comes from the Lord, the Spirit (2 Cor. 3:18).

Read the verse a few times. Let the picture sink in. To be sure, there are problems of translation and interpretation. For example, should we read "beholding" or "reflecting" (like a mirror), or perhaps "reflecting by beholding"? And how are we to understand the double reference, "the Lord, the Spirit"?

According to rules of interpretation that Paul had learned in his rabbinic schooling, he sees the Spirit where the text refers to "the Lord." He concludes: Where the text in Exodus 34 reads LORD, I read Spirit—and where the Spirit is there is freedom. And God's gracious sunshine, the Spirit, can work healing without obstruction as once in the beginning, long before Moses on Sinai, in the very beginning, when God created the world and the Spirit gave life and breath.

We know that Paul had the creation story at the back of his mind, when he wrote this part of his letter. His words came to be shaped by his remembering the story of the creation of humanity in the very image and likeness of God, and by breathing the Spirit into earthen vessels. For when Paul concludes the description of his ministry as marked by the Spirit, he refers to his call by alluding to the creation story: "For it is the God who said, 'Let light shine out of darkness,' who has shone in our hearts to give the light of the knowledge of the glory of God in the face of Christ. But we have this treasure in earthen vessels . . ." (4:6–7). It is clear that Paul here says "we" but thinks primarily of his own experiences—yet suggesting them as a challenging model for his disciples. Remember how he often said, "be you my imitators." It is as if we were with Paul journeying on the road to Damascus where, according to the Book of Acts, a "light from heaven flashed about him" (9:3). The call that he heard as he fell to the ground was to "the gospel of the glory of Christ who is the image of God" (the *imago Dei,* the "icon of God," 2 Cor. 4:4).

## The glory and the down payment

It is also worth noting that the word "glory" *(doxa,* as in "doxology") comes again and again in the exuberant language of this section. The word has a number of meanings and connotations, many of them pointing towards the radiant quality of the divine realm, and that is well expressed by the New English Bible which translates it as "the divine splendor." In the Greek of the synagogues in Paul's time, *doxa* sometimes had a specific meaning. It referred to that "glory" that humanity had received by being created in the image of God. We know that Paul speaks of "the glory" exactly in that sense, for example, when he speaks of how we "fall short of the glory of God" and hence are in need of the justification by faith

79

that Paul preaches among the Gentiles
(Rom. 3:23). Or when he describes how
"the creation itself will be set free from its
bondage to decay and obtain the freedom of
the glory of the children of God" (Rom.
8:21). So freedom and liberty are qualities of
the restored humanity, and the Spirit is the
first installment, "the first-fruit" (8:23), the
"down payment" towards this redemption.
I say "down payment" or "first installment,"
not "pledge" or "guarantee" as one often
translates the word Paul uses *(arrabon,* 2
Cor. 1:22, 5:5; cf. Eph. 1:14). What is the
difference? A pledge or guarantee is a
promise, a sheet of paper, but the down payment is real cash. The Holy Spirit is not
"spiritual" in the sense of being just a
promise, it is a piece of the divine energy
itself at work in us and among us, the first
installment of our ultimate redemption. And
the Holy Spirit witnesses with our human
spirit that we are children of God (Rom.
8:16).

**With unveiled faces**

We have wandered around for a while in the Pauline garden of thought. We have done so in order to become sensitive to the various motifs and insights and experiences that I find coming together in such a remarkable way in that radiant verse already quoted. As we pray the Holy Spirit to come with its full power of transformation and inspiration towards the renewal of the whole creation, that very verse gives us a glimpse of how it works, how the Holy Spirit works in us and among us. Let us read the verse once more:

> And we all, with unveiled faces, beholding the glory of the Lord, are being changed into that same image from glory to glory; for this comes from the Lord, the Spirit (2 Cor. 3:18).

Those words breathe healing. I think of a hymn much loved in my tradition, written by one of the spiritual teachers of the eighteenth century in Germany, Gerhard Tersteegen (original title *Gott ist gegenwärtig):*

81

Light of light eternal,
All things penetrating,
For your rays our soul is waiting.
As the tender flowers willingly unfolding,
To the sun their faces holding:
Even so, may we grow
Letting grace renew us
And your life imbue us.

Or, we are reminded of the treasures of
Orthodox spirituality and theology, for it was
and is the Eastern churches that developed
deep insights into this mystery of *theosis* and
glorification: God became human that we
may regain the *imago Dei,* the glory of the
children of God.

We have seen earlier how especially the
Gospel of John loves to describe the faith in
what we called "biological" terms, that is, as
a strengthening, renewal, and growth of life,
the new birth and the new flow of energy
which is the Holy Spirit. Now we see how
Paul understands our redemption also as that
restoration of the divine life. And it is exactly

when Paul thinks about the Spirit that his thought and experience move in such furrows.

When we pray: *Come, Holy Spirit—Renew the Whole Creation,* then we should be bold, daring to live without the veils of false timidity. We should expose ourselves to that transformation. Without masks we stand in God's healing sun, convalescing, being made whole by the Spirit.

# FIVE

# The Holy Spirit and the Whole *Oikoumene*

The church is a community invigorated by the Spirit for the mending of the whole creation. I sometimes think of the church as a laboratory in which we offer our lives as guinea-pigs for the kingdom of God. In many ways, that is the prophetic vision of the role of God's covenant with Israel. That covenant was the calling to be "a peculiar people" (Deut. 14:2 *et al.*), a distinct minority with a mission. The prophet Isaiah sees that mission as Israel's calling to be "a light to the Gentiles" (Isa. 49:6, cf. 42:6, 51:4), a witness to the oneness of God and the moral order of the universe. It is this minority model, this "laboratory" model, that has given Israel the deep insight that it is quite possible for human beings to be fully acceptable to God without believing and behaving as the Jews. Jews never thought it to be God's hottest dream that everybody become a Jew. In that faith Israel has a mighty lesson to teach Christians who, in the zeal of their faith, often appear to have lost that humble perspective.

In a pluralistic world, in the whole *Oikoumene,* it is important for us to remember that Christianity in its early history also understood itself as a "peculiar people" (as the KJV rightly said in 1 Pet. 2:9). In Luke's Christmas story the old Simeon remembers the verse from Isaiah as he sings of Jesus' future mission as being "a light to lighten the Gentiles" (2:32). The imagery used in the Sermon on the Mount is distinctly minority language and laboratory language: the salt of the earth and the light of the world. A little salt goes a long way, and nobody wants the world to become a salt mine. And the famous word about the Christians as light makes the point abundantly clear: "Let your light so shine among people that they see your good deeds and give glory to your father who is in heaven" (Matt. 5:16). The aim seems to be not so much the victory of Christianity but rather that the life of the disciples will give people reason to praise God. Thus the early Christians understood themselves as a new "peculiar people," a new laboratory for the mending of the creation. In Jesus Christ this new people is not based on ethnic identity as is Israel, but brought together from people of all nations, gathered by the Spirit around Jesus Christ as Lord and Savior. It is to be a distinct minority, but not confined to any land or culture.

As such a distinct and peculiar people we are called to find our place and role of serving God within the whole *Oikoumene*. The ecumenical movement of the churches came to inherit a very limited application of that Greek term. The word means "the inhabited world." It would be both arrogant and silly for Christians to claim the word *Oikoumene* for ourselves. We share our world with people of many living faiths and many who

claim to have none—all created in the image
of God and thereby our sisters and brothers
in the family of common humanity. For this
wider ecumenism—the real one—the Spirit
gives both mandate and energy.

When we call on the Holy Spirit to renew
the whole creation, we become aware that
God's Spirit permeates the whole cosmos
and the whole *Oikoumene* in ways that cannot be controlled or manipulated by us. The
Spirit surely "bloweth where it listeth" (John
3:8). That has always been disconcerting to
orderly religious souls. Remember how
Joshua, "the minister of Moses," asked
Moses to forbid unauthorized prophets.
Moses' response echoes through the ages:
"Are you jealous for my sake? Would that all
the LORD's people were prophets, that the
LORD would put his Spirit upon them"
(Num. 11:28). What a liberating generosity
and what a wonderful unmasking of that
strange "jealousy" for God's sake that cannot rejoice in the work of the Spirit in the
whole *Oikoumene!* Jesus seems to have had

that episode in mind when his disciples acted in a similar manner. It was then that Jesus said: "Those who are not against us are for us" (Mark 9:38–41). We quote the opposite saying more easily (Matt. 12:30). We seem to like the *either/or* more than the *both/and*.

The Holy Spirit, the one and ever same eternal Spirit, will enable us to think "both-and" in many situations where we excel in "either-or." We shall become familiar with the ways in which:

—the Spirit as Teacher renews the faith of the church *and* the intellectual quest of humanity;

—the Spirit as Unifier renews the love of the church *and* the solidarity of humanity;

—the Spirit as Liberator renews the justice of the church *and* the moral energy of humanity;

—the Spirit as Vivifier renews the hope of the church *and* the aspirations of humanity.[1]

---

[1] See Philip J. Rosano, S.J., "The Mission of the Spirit Within and Beyond the Church," in *The Ecumenical Review*, Vol. 41, No. 3, July 1989.

So we must learn to sing our song to Jesus Christ with abandon, without telling negative stories about others. For it is simply not true that our faith and our devotion would be weakened by recognizing the insights and the beauty and the truths in other faiths. As we suggested earlier (in our discussion of Paul's ecumenism in Corinth), such perceptions are secular, worldly, and carnal, treating God as an object for philosophical arguments. The spiritual perception is not bound by that "zero-sum" reasoning where a plus for the one is a minus for the other. I do not need to hate all other women to prove that I love my wife. Quite the contrary. The very attitude of contempt or condescension or negativism towards others pollutes the love of one's own. It is not improper to apply Paul's principle of *agape,* of mutual esteem, also to the whole *Oikoumene,* to the wider ecumenism which by the promptings of the Spirit will increasingly call for our attention.

I sometimes wonder what will happen to all our adjectives when God mends and redeems and restores the Creation. For in the ultimate sense there can be no "Christian" or "Muslim" truth. Things are either true or not true. And to speak about the "Christian God" is really careless short-hand for "the conceptions and perceptions of God that scholars have found in Christianity." But when we worship God, then there is only one God, however perceived through time and space. God beyond adjectives and partial claims, is not that what those famous words point to: "God is spirit and those who worship him must worship him in spirit and in truth" (John 4:24)? Or when we are told that in the heavenly city there was no temple to be seen, for its temple is the Lord God Almighty and the Lamb—the sacrifice to end all sacrifices (Rev. 21:22)? Or when Paul reflects on how ultimately Jesus Christ will lay down his power before God "and thus God will be all in all" (1 Cor. 15:28)?

Towards that glorious end we pray without conditions and reservations, energized already now by some of the freedom of the glory of the children of God:

*Come, Holy Spirit—Renew the Whole Creation.*